KT-116-748

Starting Over

Bob Gass

Bridge-Logos *Publishers*

Gainesville, Florida 32614 USA

Bible translations (abbreviations) used:

NIV   New International Version
Copyright © 1973,1978,1984 by the International Bible Society. Used by
permission of Zondervan Bible Publishers.
TLB   The Living Bible
TM   The Message
Copyright © by Eugene H. Peterson, 1993,1994,1995. Used by permission of
NavPress Publishing Group
NAS   New American Standard
Copyright © 1960,1962,1963,1968,1971,1972,1973,1975,1977
by the Lockman Foundation Used by permission.
KJV   King James Version
CEV   Contemporary English Version
AMP   Amplied Bible
NLT   New Living Translation

Note: All quotations are taken from the *King James Version,* unless otherwise
notated.

Starting Over

Copyright © 2000 by Bob Gass
Library of Congress Catalog Card Number: 00-105357
International Standard Book Number: 0-88270-828-7

Bridge-Logos *Publishers*
P.O. Box 141630
Gainesville, FL 32614, USA
http://www.bridgelogos.com

Starting Over

Table of Contents

Preface

Acknowledgements

Many of the principles found in these pages were inspired by John Maxwell's great book *Failing Forward* (Nelson Publishers). In it he points out that the difference between winners and losers is their perception of failure, and their response to it. Then he challenges us to fail early, fail often, and always fail forward.

It's the stuff we need to hear—every day —if we are to overcome our fear of failing, learn from our mistakes, and go on to fulfill our destiny.

Preface

Failing doesn't mean I'm a failure; it just means I have not yet succeeded. It doesn't mean I've accomplished nothing; it just means I've learned something. It doesn't mean I've been a fool; it just means I've had the courage to take a risk. It doesn't mean I'm inferior; it just means I'm not perfect. It doesn't mean I've wasted my time; it just means I have a reason to start over. It doesn't mean I should give up; it just means I have to try harder. It doesn't mean I'll never make it; it just means I need more patience. It doesn't mean God has abandoned me; it just means He has a better idea!

Chapter One

David Purse Jr.

During some of the worst days of the violence in Northern Ireland, a series of "reprisal killings" took place that targeted the most innocent and the most defenseless. Fear spread over the province like a dark cloud. The locals referred to it as the "tit-for-tat killings."

One Saturday afternoon, on January 12, 1979, a car pulled up outside Seaview Soccer Stadium in north Belfast, and a hooded man stepped out with a rifle. At point blank range, he pumped four bullets into the head of David Purse Sr., a policeman, and the father of three little boys. The gunman disappeared into a safehouse nearby, and to my knowledge he's never been found.

Besides being a police officer, David Purse Sr. was also the Sunday school superintendent at the 3,000 member Metropolitan Tabernacle in Belfast. As crowds gathered three days later for the funeral, Dr. James McConnell, his pastor, wept openly over the loss of a husband, a father, a member, a friend, and a country ripped apart.

Five years later I met David Purse Jr. at the spot where his Dad had been slain. He'd agreed to do an interview with me for a television network in the United States. As the camera focused in on us, I asked this seventeen-year-old to take me back to that day and tell me how he felt.

Looking at me intensely he said, "Hate; raw hate! It consumed me for months. It was all I thought about day and night. The only time I felt better was when I heard or read in the newspaper, that some of the *'other side'* had been killed too.

"I thought constantly about joining a paramilitary organization, getting a gun and doing to them what they had done to me.

"Inside I was raging; I knew I was wrong, but I didn't know how to change it. I prayed, but I felt like the Psalmist when he said, "My prayer returned into mine own bosom" (Psalm 35:13). It was like a fever inside me that had to run its course and then break.

"Six months later—it did!

"Up until this time my goal had been to attend Queen's University and study medicine. Yet I was aware of something pulling me in a different direction—the ministry.

"I was scheduled to be baptized one weekend, and in an attempt to prepare my heart for the event I tried to pray again; but it was useless. That's when I heard a voice say to me, *'David Purse, the hate that's in your heart right now, is exactly the same kind that was in the hearts of the men who murdered your Dad. So what does that make you?'*

The words were like a sledgehammer breaking a rock. That night, David Purse Jr. reached his breaking point—and his turning point.

"It was as though a big hand had reached down into a bathtub filled with rage and pulled the stopper," he told me. "Slowly the bitterness started draining away, and I began to understand the words of Job, a man who had lost a lot more than me 'You shall forget your misery; you shall remember it as waters that pass away . . . though there be darkness, it shall be as the morning'" (Job 11:16-17).

Morning was dawning for David Purse Jr.

As we finished the interview that gray Saturday afternoon, he looked at me and said, "I have asked God for two things; first, to preach the Gospel of peace from one end of this land to the other. Second, to meet the man who murdered my Dad; not to exact revenge, but to tell him about God's love, for that's the only hope *any* of us have."

A few years later at the age of 21, David accepted his first pastorate in one of the border towns that separates Northern and Southern Ireland. It was a terrorist stronghold, and the last place on earth he would ever have picked. But God picked it for him.

Of the one hundred people in his congregation, all of whom he had grown to love dearly, 99% were from *"the other side."*

David Purse Jr. now lives in England with his wife, Donna, and their three boys, and pastors two growing churches. Every day he touches *hundreds* of lives with God's love.

But it only happened because he decided to do two things: (1) forgive, and keep on forgiving, until the past could neither hold nor hurt him any more, (2) start over and take control of his life.

You can do that too—if you really want to!

Chapter Two

Three Life-Changing Principles

"I do not have time to tell about Gideon, Barak, Samson, Jephthah..." (Hebrews 11:32, NIV).

You ask, "Who's Jephthah?" One of the greatest military heroes in Israel's history. But getting there wasn't easy.

His Mom was a prostitute; his Dad was promiscuous; his half-brothers were hateful and threw him out of the house before he could inherit a penny of the family's wealth. When he turned for help to the city fathers, the one group he thought would stand by him, they played politics and slammed the door in his face.

Broken but not defeated, he went up into the hill country to a place called Tob. The name means *"good."* How remarkable! He discovered purpose in the midst of his pain. Out of devastation he found direction—and you can too.

Even though he had been reduced to living in a cave he refused to live like a "victim." Instead he used the time to prepare for his future. He began recruiting and training an army that would fight a decisive battle and ultimately make him a legend. It's interesting how it happened.

One day when the Ammonites attacked Israel, the city fathers, yes the same ones who turned their backs on him years before, came hat-in-hand, begging him for help. What would *you* have done?

Jephthah didn't just help them; he put his life on the line for them!

His rag-tag army leveled 20 enemy cities as the Ammonite hordes went down before his forces like stubble in a storm. As a reward, he was made the youngest governor in his nation's history, and he ended up in the Bible's "Hall of Fame" with men like Gideon, Samson and David *(see Hebrews, Chapter 11).*

So what's *your* excuse for quitting?

Before you mention it, step on to the scales with Jephthah. He refused to let his past rob him of his future. Instead of curling up into a ball of self-pity and resentment, he rose up and took control of his life. That meant overcoming his beginnings and starting again. You say, "How did he do it?" By observing three life-changing principles. Here they are:

1) The answer to old relationships—is new ones.

One day God said to the prophet Samuel, "How long wilt thou mourn for Saul? Fill thine horn with oil and go . . .for I have provided" (1 Samuel 16:1). Samuel grieved the loss of King Saul for so long that God had to visit him and tell him, "It's time to move on."

There's a step beyond death; it's called burial. It separates the dead from the living, and the past from the future. Some of us get through it faster than others and some of us never do. We talk only of the past, because we stopped living at a certain point years ago.

Any time you discuss the past as though it was the present, it's because you've allowed the past to steal the present right out of your hands. Don't do it! Rise up and take it back! Listen again to what God told Samuel, "Go . . . for I have provided."

Did you hear that? God's provided *everything* you need to start over!

Here's your choice: you can keep lamenting what nobody can change, or you can start living in the present and begin to plan for the future. God says, "I have provided." There are friends who are just waiting to be part of your life the moment you decide to live again. Let that sink in!

Stop reliving events that are dead and gone! Stop arguing with people who aren't even listening! Take all your time, your love, and your energy, and give it to the future, for it's time to move on.

2) The answer to pain is purpose!

Are you battling loneliness and depression? The first step out is to find a cause greater than you, and give yourself to it. When the focus changes from you to others, your life will begin to take an upswing.

If self-centeredness has kept you from "getting over yourself," examine your attitude, and determine to make *others* your priority. Start by asking yourself the following questions, either at the beginning or at the end of each day:

     a. Into whom am I pouring my life?

     b. Who am I helping who can't give me back anything in return?

     c. Who am I encouraging daily?

3) The answer to resentment is a commitment to walk in love and forgiveness.

One day Peter said to Jesus, "Lord, how oft shall my brother sin against me, and I forgive him? till seven times?" Jesus replied, *"Until seventy times seven"* (Matthew 18:21-22).

Wow! Do you realize what Jesus told Peter to do? If you're awake sixteen hours a day, that means forgiving your brother—*every two minutes!* That's not an act, it's an attitude. It means forgive, and keep on forgiving, until it loses its power over you.

During the last days of the Berlin Wall, some hard-liners in the East drove a truck filled with garbage over into the West and dumped it just inside the Wall. Instead of retaliating, a few wiser and cooler heads filled a truck with food and humanitarian aid, drove it over to the East, and stacked it up neatly just inside the Wall.

They also left a note that read, *"Each gives what he has to give!"*

If garbage is what you've got, garbage is what you'll give. If love and forgiveness is what you've got, love and forgiveness is what you'll give. The choice is yours. Furthermore, your future depends on it being the right choice!

Forgiveness is not for the benefit of others— it's for *your* benefit! Until you can forgive the offense and release the person who hurt you, you can't move on.

Why waste another moment of your life living that way?

Chapter Three

The Rearview Mirror

One day I stopped to offer help to a lady whose car had run off the road into a ditch. Fortunately, she wasn't hurt, and her car had suffered only a few minor scrapes and dents.

"What happened?" I asked her.

Half embarrassed and half amused she replied, "Instead of watching the road ahead of me, I was looking in my rearview mirror, freshening my makeup." Then she laughed and said, "I think next time I'll pull off the road before I try that."

A few minutes later, I watched as a big truck with flashing yellow lights hauled her out of the drainage culvert, and towed her to the nearest service station. As they disappeared, I had this illuminating thought: *There's no way to go forward, if you're looking at what's behind. If you do, you'll end up in a ditch for sure!*

This lady got out of her ditch pretty quickly and with only minimal damage. Some of us seem to spend our whole lives trying to get out of ours!

Chapter Four

Lessons From My Mother

My father died when I was 12. He left without saying goodbye.

My older brother Neil and my little sister Ruth and I were excited because he was coming home from the hospital the next day, after being treated for coronary thrombosis. As far as we knew he had been given "a clean bill of health."

That summer evening as my Mom sat holding his hand, he was his old cheerful self, telling jokes and keeping her entertained. She adored him.

Suddenly, without a moment's warning, a blood clot dislodged, traveled to his brain, and he fell lifeless across the bed. It happened in seconds.

She screamed, but he didn't move. Unable to comprehend or accept what had happened, she grabbed one of the attending physicians and shook him like a rag doll, shouting, "Tell me he's not dead; tell me he's not dead."

She was a widow at 40.

For the next two years she struggled to start over. More than once she argued with God, "Why did you take him? I needed him more than you did." She especially hated the term "widow" and refused to let anyone call her it.

For months after he had gone she would see him so vividly in her dreams that she would actually get out of bed and go to meet him. But when her hand touched the bedroom door, she would awaken and dissolve into tears.

I was only thirteen at the time, but I remember that helpless feeling as I lay in the bedroom next to hers, listening to her muffled sobs.

The government gave her "a widow's pension" of nine dollars a week. Even though it wouldn't feed the four of us for more than a day or two, she tithed. The thought of doing otherwise would never have entered her mind.

Often I'd say to her, "You can't afford to." But she'd just smile and say, "I can't afford *not* to. Tithing is not about money it's about obedience. When I give God His portion, I can go to Him with confidence and know that He'll meet all of my needs. You see, I don't have to do anything to earn His love; He gives that freely to us all. But I do have to do certain things if I want to enjoy His blessings." Then she would add, "We may live a hand to mouth existence, but always remember son, it's God's hand to our mouth."

She taught me three things about giving that still govern my life.

First, the seed you sow will never leave your life. It simply moves from where you are today, to where you'll be tomorrow; but when you get there it will no longer be the seed you planted, but the harvest you need. She believed that as long as she kept on sowing, she would keep on reaping— and she did.

Second, she taught me that God will never ask you for something you don't have, but He'll always ask you for something you'd like to keep. She knew that giving proves you've conquered greed. It also proves you've conquered the fear of lack.

17

Third, she taught me that you always have enough to create what you need. She'd say, "When what I have is not enough, I just make it a seed. The moment I put that seed into God's hands, my next harvest begins."

The things I learned from watching her have impacted me more than all the books I've ever read, and all the sermons I've ever listened to.

Some of the kids I grew up with on the streets of Belfast joined sectarian organizations, and ended up dead or in prison. But she took God in one hand and us in the other, and announced, "As for me and my house, we will serve the Lord."

It paid off; today both of her sons are in the ministry and her daughter is a Christian writer!

It took a few years for her to get back on her feet after the loss of my Dad. But when she finally came out of that valley, she became a friend to the friendless, a champion to the underdog, and a support system for ministers and missionaries everywhere.

She also prayed for me. At the most broken and devastated moments of my life, when I wasn't sure I'd make it, I believe it was her praying that pulled me through. She said she was "standing in the gap" for me. I'm convinced that she had a direct line to God; when she talked, He listened, and things changed.

As I sat down to write this chapter I asked myself what it was that enabled her to overcome her grief, poverty, and oppressive surroundings, and go on to make such a difference in the lives of so many others?

Three things came to mind almost immediately.

First, she lived by the Scriptures. She had a verse for everything—and it could be aggravating. If we didn't treat the dog right, she'd say, "A righteous man regardeth the life of his beast." Or if we talked negatively she'd say, "You'll be snared by the words of your mouth." The woman was a walking Bible!

One of her favorite verses was, "Faith cometh by hearing, and hearing by the Word of God" (Romans 10:17). By soaking herself in the scriptures each day she found the faith and the courage she needed to overcome every difficulty.

Second, she gave her life to others. She knew there was no solution in blame, and no healing in self-interest. If you had nowhere to go, you could always come to our house.

I'm moved now as I recall her compassion, but I wasn't too impressed with it at the time. Not that she ever consulted me about it. If I'd even *thought* of saying anything negative about the people who lived in our guest room, (most of whom I thought were weird) she'd throw me a glance and say, "In as much as ye have done it to the least of one of these My brethren, ye have done it unto Me."

By focusing her attention on others rather than herself, she found healing, self-worth, and direction for her life.

Third, her favorite place was church. There she built a network of friends who celebrated her victories and supported her in her struggles. Every time the doors were open she was there—and so was I!

Today I meet a lot of parents who tell me, "My children don't want to go to church," and I imagine their children are probably in their middle to late teens. But then I discover that some of them are as young as 10, 11 or 12, and I think to myself, "How can that be?" I never got an *invitation* to church in my life. Nor did I get to vote on going, because we didn't live in a democracy. She'd just look at me and say, "Young man if you want to see your next birthday—you'll be in God's house!"

Now being in "God's House" didn't just mean Sunday morning—that would have been fine. No, for me it also meant *two* Sunday Schools on Sunday afternoon as well; one Presbyterian and the other Brethren. When I pointed out that all my friends just went to *one* Sunday School, so how come I had to go to *two*, she'd smile and say, "It's a back-up plan, in case you weren't listening the first time around!"

After the second Sunday School we had a quick supper. It resembled the ancient Passover meal where they ate standing up, their staff in their hand, their loins girt about them, and ready to move at a moment's notice. Our situation was similar, because we had to catch two connecting buses to make it on time for the seven o'clock evangelistic service.

I liked that service because they had lively music and a band. Furthermore, at the ripe old age of 12, they made me the church drummer. Now I'm not sure what the fabled *McNamara's Band* sounded like, but I'm told that what it lacked in skill, it made up for in enthusiasm. That was us.

The night I joined it, my mother took me aside and in stern tones reminded me that mine was now "a high calling." When my friends at school heard about my high calling, they promptly nicknamed me "Moses" and "Abraham."

But the meeting I dreaded most was the Monday night prayer meeting, which lasted for hours. I thought it was "the tribulation period" spoken of in the Book of Revelation, and the church had to go through it every week. The same people standing up, praying the same prayers year after year. If they had dropped dead in the middle of their prayer, I could have finished it off for them.

She also made me attend the Wednesday night Bible study and the Friday night youth service. And if she could find a series of "revival meetings," I was in church *every night*.

While my friends were playing soccer and going to the "flicks," I was being "planted in the courts of the Lord."

Even though I love and appreciate it today, the church I grew up in wasn't a lot of fun. We weren't permitted to go to the movies; although when television came, the same people who preached against them, now watched them in their own home.

I never asked about this, because such questions were considered a form of rebellion.

We were also warned against going to football games, because that was "mixing with the world." I really wondered about that one. Was their darkness stronger than our light? I think the idea was that being seen in worldly places with worldly people could ruin your testimony, especially if it looked like you were having a good time.

We also preached against money—and it worked; people with money never came to our church! The fact that we couldn't afford a decent building, pay a pastor, put an ad in the local newspaper, or support a missionary, didn't give us a second thought.

One of the favorite targets of our preaching was against ladies who wore makeup. God help them! I never quite understood it, for even an old barn looks better with a little paint on it. In our services we'd sing:

Dare to be a Daniel, dare to stand alone,
Stay outside the chemist's shop,
and call your face your own.

Furthermore, we preached against smoking, drinking, gambling, and adultery. Especially adultery, because I think they were afraid that it could lead to dancing!

You may not believe this, but we even preached against eating pork. Honestly! You haven't lived until you've heard two hundred people clapping, playing tambourines, and singing:

Keep the food laws, they are good laws,
Praise the Lord I'm feeling fine,
since I left off eating swine.

My younger sister, Ruth, was part of a group that sang in the "open-air meetings" on Friday nights. The strategy here was to catch the drunks coming out of the pubs at closing time, which was 10 P.M.

Because of the lateness of the hour the only musician the group could find was a guy called "Shuey." He played the chanter. It was an instrument that looked like bag pipes without the bag, and it produced a wailing, forlorn sound.

One of their favorite numbers for trying on the drunks was:

There are two things God doth detest,
High-heel shoes and a low-neck dress.
I ain't a gonna grieve my Lord no more.

One particular night the spot they chose for their open-air meeting was right beneath a music school, which met upstairs and offered evening classes to its students. It was a serious institution.

Again Shuey and the chanters struck up:
This is one thing I will not do,
I will not stand in a cinema queue.
I ain't a gonna grieve my Lord no more.

The words and the music wafted their way through the windows of the music school upstairs, bringing all serious study to a screeching halt.

Within moments the school's director appeared with the face of a thundercloud, and informed them that not only were they disrupting his class, but furthermore, if *any* of his students *ever* produced such a sound he'd close the entire place down.

Upon hearing that, Shuey told the chanters, "It's just an attack of the devil," and moved them on to the next corner, and the next group of defenseless drunks.

Anyway, that's enough about "the old days."

In spite of all these humorous memories, I treasure the foundations that were laid, and the truths that were taught to me during those formative years. They've been like an anchor that's held me in the biggest storms of my life.

Because I watched my mother beat the odds and start over again, I was able to do the same thing when my life fell apart years later.

Chapter Five

How Big Is Your Mistake Quota?

Everybody fails. The winners are just the ones that keep getting back up again!

Really, the only way to be a loser is to fail and quit; or fail and not learn from it; or fail and not look beyond it; or fail and let it define you as a failure.

Listen carefully to these words, "For time would fail me to tell of Gideon and of Barak, and of Samson, and of Jephthah; of David also, and Samuel, and of the prophets: who through faith subdued kingdoms, wrought righteousness, obtained promises, stopped the mouths of lions, quenched the violence of the fire, escaped the edge of the sword, *out of weakness were made strong.*" (Hebrews 11:33-34).

Note the words "out of weakness were made strong". Built into every painful experience you've ever had, is the wisdom you need to start over and do it better the next time.

In *Leadership Magazine*, J. Wallace Hamilton says, "The increase of suicides, alcoholics, and even some forms of nervous breakdowns, is evidence that many people are training for success without ever being trained to handle failure. Yet failure is far more common than success, poverty is far more prevalent than wealth, and disappointment is far more normal than arrival."

Only when you can look failure in the eye, experience it and move beyond it, will you succeed.

In the *Psychology of Achievement*, Brian Tracy tells of four millionaires who made their fortunes by the age of 35. What's notable about them is that all four tried an average of *seventeen* different things before they found the one that made them successful!

Imagine that! They tried and failed and changed—*sixteen times*—before they found what worked for them. That's what it takes, an attitude that refuses to quit!

We are too quick to judge things as failures when they're just learning experiences. Knowing what *doesn't* work, moves you one step closer to knowing what *does*.

Thomas Edison said, "Many of life's failures are just people who did not realize how close they were to success when they gave up." The key is having the commitment to move through your failures, learning as you go, and taking hold of the success that lies just beyond them.

Failure is like fertilizer; it's the stuff success grows in.

Herbert Brocknow has a great saying: "The fellow who never makes a mistake takes his orders from the one who does." When you can allow yourself to fail, you're also allowing yourself permission to succeed. You can't experience one without the other.

Chuck Braun of Idea Connection Systems gives each of his trainees *"a mistake quota."* It works like this: each student can make thirty mistakes during a training session and have nothing to worry about. If he uses up all thirty, Chuck gives him *another* thirty. And the result? Suddenly his trainees begin to think of mistakes as "a creative process," and see them as an essential part of the learning curve.

Before Edison gave the world incandescent light, he conducted one thousand failed experiments. When a reporter asked him how he felt about failing one-thousand times he replied, *"I didn't fail a thousand times. The electric light bulb was just a one thousand step process."* What an answer!

Sadly, most of us grew up in a culture where failure was unacceptable, and it was usually rewarded with embarrassment and condemnation. That perception *must* be changed before you can begin to move forward.

Chapter Six

Keep Bouncing Back!

Do you feel like a failure? Would you like to break out of your negative thinking patterns? If so, look at an area of your life where you keep failing and do the following:

Check your expectations! Write them down, and then ask yourself—Are they realistic? Do I expect to do everything perfectly or succeed on the first try? How many mistakes will I allow myself before I succeed? Then adjust your expectations to reality.

Try something different! Brainstorm at least twenty or thirty new methods and then try at least half of them. If the first ten don't work, just tell yourself, "O.K., now I know that it's at least an eleven-step process"—and keep going!

Use your strengths! Utilize your best skills and strengths and then learn to "staff your weakness." There are gifted people around you whose dreams will come true by helping to make yours come true. Look for them.

Learn to bounce back! No matter how many times you fall down, get back up and start over. Paul J. Meyer says, "Ninety percent of all those who fail are not actually defeated. They simply quit."

Do you remember the Wright Brothers? They were the two bicycle mechanics who pioneered the first airplane.

But did you also know that Dr. Samuel Langley, a professor of mathematics and astronomy at the Smithsonian Institute, was expected to do it before them? This brilliant scientist published books on the subject *ten years* before the Wright brothers even thought of flying their first plane. His experiments achieved such a high level of success, that the U.S. War Department even funded him.

But on October 8, 1903 when Langley tried to fly his first bi-plane, it finished up in the water, not more than 50 yards from where it had taken off.

The *New York Times* blasted him and called it "A ridiculous fiasco." They wrote, "Man might fly one day—perhaps one to ten million years from now."

But Langley was able to ignore their criticism and stay focused.

Two months later he tried again. And again he was unsuccessful. This time the wing supports broke as the plane took off, and it plunged upside down into a river. The pilot almost died.

The newspapers labeled it, "Langley's Folly." Again the *New York Times* led the way; "We hope that Professor Langley will not put his substantial greatness in further peril by continuing to waste his time and money."

This time Langley couldn't bounce back!

Soon after this he wrote, "I have brought to a close the portion of the work, which seemed to be specially mine. For the next stage the world may look to others." Deeply discouraged he gave up his life's dream without seeing one of his planes in the air.

Nine days later, Orville and Wilbur Wright, with no education and no funds, flew their plane, *Flyer I,* over the sands of Kitty Hawk and into the history books.

A little over two years after his failure, Langley suffered a stroke and died. Sadly, while most of the world has heard of the Wright Brothers, he is almost unknown.

Why did Langley finally fail? Because he considered his failure to be final! He didn't have a big enough "mistake quota."

J. I. Packer says, "A moment of conscious triumph makes one feel that after this nothing really matters; a moment of realized disaster makes one feel that this is the end of everything. *But neither feeling is realistic, for neither event is really what it is felt to be.*"

Chapter Seven

Keep Believing In Yourself!

Erma Bombeck's first job was as a copy girl at *Dayton Journal-Herald*. In college her guidance counselor told her to "forget about writing" because she didn't have the talent for it. But she refused to listen, and after she got her degree in English, she began writing for the obituary column and the women's page.

Besides wanting to be a writer, one of her greatest desires was to be a mother. But the doctors told her she was incapable of having children. Did that stop her? No way! She went out and adopted a daughter. Two years later, to her delight, she conceived.

Even that brought problems. In four years she experienced four pregnancies but only two of her babies survived.

In 1964 she convinced the editor of a small neighborhood newspaper, the *Kettering-Oakwood Times*, to let her write a weekly humor column. Her starting salary was $3.00 a week. The next year she was offered a chance to write a column, three-times-a-week, for her old employer, the *Dayton Journal Herald*.

That was the break she needed! She seized the opportunity and made the most of it.

By 1967, she was so successful that her column was syndicated in more than *nine hundred newspapers*. For the next thirty years she wrote words that lifted the spirits and enriched the lives of people everywhere.

During that time she published fifteen books, and was recognized as one of the 25 most influential women in America. She appeared frequently on *Good Morning America*, was featured on the cover of *Time*, received The American Cancer Society's Medal of Honor, and was awarded fifteen honorary degrees.

But during that same time, she also experienced incredible challenges and setbacks, including breast cancer, a mastectomy, and kidney failure.

She shared her experiences like this; "When I speak at college commencements I tell everyone, 'I'm up here and you're down there, not because of my successes, but because of my failures.'

"Then I proceed to spin them all off—a comedy album that sold two copies in Beirut. A sitcom that lasted about as long as a doughnut in our house. A Broadway play that never saw Broadway, and book signings where I attracted two people—one who wanted directions to the restroom, and another who wanted to buy the desk I was sitting at.

"What you have to tell yourself is, 'I'm not a failure; I just failed at doing something.' *There's a big difference!*

"Personally and careerwise, it's been a corduroy road. I've buried babies, lost parents, had cancer and worried over kids. The trick is to put it all in perspective, and that's what I do for a living."

Every great success has struggled with failure—everyone of them!

Mozart was told by Emperor Ferdinand that his opera, *The Marriage of Figaro,* was "far too noisy and had far too many notes." Van Gogh sold only *one* painting during his lifetime, yet today his smallest painting brings millions of dollars. Einstein was considered unteachable as a child. His schoolteacher in Munich told him he would "never amount to anything."

Yet they kept believing in themselves and refused to accept failure.

Author Leo Buscaglia was a great admirer of television cooking expert Julia Child. He said, "I just love her attitude." She says, 'Tonight we're going to make a soufflé!' And then she beats this and whisks that, and she drops things on the floor, and does all these wonderful human things. Then she takes the soufflé and throws it in the oven and talks to you for a while. Finally, she says, 'Now it's ready!' But when she opens the oven, the soufflé just falls flat as a pancake. But does she panic or burst into tears? No! She just smiles and says, *'Well, you can't win them all. Bon appetite!'*

If you want to succeed, the secret is not to let *any single incident* color your view of yourself!

Chapter Eight

Winners And Losers!

In 1954 the Milwaukee Braves and the Cincinnati Reds played each other on the opening day of major league baseball.

Each team had a rookie making his first appearance. The rookie who played for the Reds hit four doubles and helped his team to win. The rookie who played for the Braves didn't hit one ball. The Reds player was Jim Greengrass, a name you've probably never heard of. The other guy, the one who didn't get a single hit, might be more familiar to you. *His name is Hank Aaron, and he went on to become the best home-run hitter in the history of the game.*

If Hank Aaron had been easily discouraged, he would have given up in defeat after his first game. But he didn't—he learned from it, practiced harder, and decided he would do better next time. *That's* what it takes to be a winner!

Have you ever heard of Dick Fosbury? He's the man who changed high-jumping history. Until he came along most high jumpers went over the bar facing it. But he developed the technique of going over headfirst with his back to the bar. His technique came to be known as "The Fosbury Flop."

Everybody, including some coaches and athletes, told him it wouldn't work. But he just smiled and thought, "Somebody has to be the first to do it, or nothing will ever change or improve."

And he did it! He won the gold medal for high jumping at the Mexico City Olympic Games in 1968—and set a new record. *Now just about every world-class high jumper uses his technique!* Why? Because he was willing to try something different, and because he refused to allow his critics to intimidate him.

Psychologist Simone Caruthers says, "Life is a series of outcomes. Sometimes the outcome is what you want. Great. Figure out what you did right, and keep doing it. Sometimes the outcome is what you don't want. Great. Figure out what you did wrong and don't do it again." Either way you win if you learn from it.

But look out! *Failure* in your past can lead to *fear* in your future!

John Maxwell points out that many people get stuck in a cycle of fear. Because they don't act, they don't gain experience. This lack of experience means they can't handle similar situations, and that ultimately feeds their fear. The *longer* this fear remains unchecked, the *harder* they have to work to break the cycle.

How do you break the cycle of fear?

Hope you'll feel different tomorrow? Wait until the circumstances become less risky? The answer is—feel the fear and do it anyway!

Are you waiting for the motivation to get you going? If you are, then read these words from a medical journal:

"Motivation is not going to strike you like lightning, and it's not something that someone else—nurse, doctor, or family member—can bestow or force on you. *The whole idea of motivation is a trap. Forget motivation. Just do it!* Exercise, lose weight, test your blood sugar, or whatever. Do it without motivation and guess what? After you start doing it, the motivation will come."

Motivation begins with a decision.

The people who possess it are called "self-starters." As soon as they start moving forward—even if that means overcoming a hundred and one negative emotions—their motivation suddenly kicks in.

Harvard psychologist Jerome Brutner says, "You're more likely to act yourself into feeling, than to feel yourself into acting." So act! Whatever it is you know you should do—start doing it!

George Bernard Shaw said, "A life spent in making mistakes is not only more honorable, but more useful than a life spent doing nothing." To break the cycle of fear, you've got to take action—you simply have to!

Recently I saw a great plaque in someone's office with these words:

"Every morning in Africa, a gazelle wakes up. It knows that it must run faster than the fastest lion or it will be killed. Every morning in Africa a lion wakes up. It knows it must outrun the slowest gazelle or it will starve to death. It doesn't matter whether you are a lion or a gazelle: When the sun comes up, you had better be running."

That just about says it all—doesn't it?

Chapter Nine

No Excuses

King Solomon said, "As a man thinketh, so is he."

How do you see yourself? As a failure? As a victim? What has made you believe that? Your family history? Your immediate circumstances? Your past experiences?

Do you find yourself making excuses and blaming others? Like the drivers who filled out police reports and offered these hilarious explanations for the car accidents in which they had been involved:

"I had been driving my car for four years when I fell asleep at the wheel and had an accident."

"I was on my way to the doctor's office with rear-end trouble when my universal joint gave way."

"The pedestrian had no idea which direction to run so I ran over him."

"The guy was all over the road, I had to swerve a number of times before hitting him."

"I pulled away from the side of the road, glanced at my mother-in-law, and drove over an embankment."

"An invisible car came out of nowhere, struck me, and vanished."

Until you quit making excuses and accept personal responsibility for your life—nothing will change. No matter how often you fall down, you're not a failure until you blame somebody else for pushing you.

John H. Holiday, the founder and editor of the *Indianapolis News*, exploded in anger one day because someone had spelled *height* as *hight*. When a worker checked the original copy and explained to Holiday that he himself had been the one who did it, the editor's response was, "Well, if that's the way I spelled it, then it must be right." *The paper misspelled the word his way for the next thirty years.* Louis Armstrong once quipped, "There are some people and if they don't know, you can't tell them."

When are you going to stop blaming others, look in the mirror and say, "I'm responsible for my life, and nobody else?"

Don't be like the dying man who said to his wife, "Dear, you've been with me through thick and thin. When I got fired, you were there. When I lost the business you were there. When my health failed you were there."

After a few moments of silence he looked up at her and said, "You know what? You're bad luck!"

You may smile, but as long as you keep blaming others and refusing to accept responsibility for yourself, you'll *never* discover how great your life could have been.

But let me say something very important right here.

It's wonderful to fall and keep getting back up again, but the idea is to *learn* from it and grow wiser!

That may happen on your third fall or your three-hundredth, but at some point the light should begin to shine. Listen carefully to this essay by Portia Nelson called , "Autobiography in Five Short Chapters. " It's a real eye-opener.

Chapter 1. I walk down the street. There is a deep hole in the sidewalk. I fall in. I am lost. I am helpless. It isn't my fault. It takes forever to find a way out.

Chapter 2. I walk down the street. There is a deep hole in the sidewalk. I pretend I don't see it. I fall in again. I can't believe I am in the same place but it isn't my fault. It still takes a long time to get out.

Chapter 3. I walk down the same street. There is a deep hole in the sidewalk. I see it is there. I still fall in. It's a habit. My eyes are open. I know where I am. It is my fault. I get out immediately.

Chapter 4. I walk down the same street. There is a deep hole in the sidewalk. I walk around it.

Chapter 5. I walk down another street.

Your mistakes are not the issue; what you learn

from them is. Built into every painful experience is the wisdom to build a better future. All you need is the right perspective, a willingness to learn, and one more thing—character!

Character means being honest enough to say you're wrong, wise enough to learn from it, and courageous enough to push your way through the pain to the next level. Character is the stuff of which enduring success is made.

It's not the size of the dog in the fight, it's the size of the fight in the dog that determines who wins. Motivation comes from a well that you already have within you. Draw from it. Protect it. Keep it constantly filled with inspiration.

Consider carefully the following words from the book of Proverbs: "Keep vigilant watch over your heart; *that's* where life starts...keep your eyes straight ahead; ignore all sideshow distractions. Watch your step, and the road will stretch out smooth before you" (Proverbs 4:23-25, TM).

The apostle Peter writes, "His divine power has given us *everything* we need . . . He has given us His very great and precious promises, so that through them you may participate in the divine nature" (2 Peter 1:3-4, NIV).

Did you get that? With God as your source, you've got *everything* you need to be successful. So make your relationship with Him a priority!

Chapter Ten

The Attitude That Overcomes!

Where did you ever get the idea that *everybody* would appreciate you? Certainly not from Jesus! He said His blessings are reserved for the "persecuted" and "reviled" (Matthew 5:11). If you have thin skin, life will give you a rough time, and your critics will find you an easy target.

Endurance is the secret —not popularity!

Look what Paul endured in order to fulfill his life's goal. Desertion by his friends, ugly letters from the Corinthians, disappointment with the Galatians, mistreatment in Philippi, mocking in Athens, imprisonment and beheading in Rome. And *you're* complaining?

From prison he writes, "Everything happening to me in this jail only serves to make Christ more accurately known, regardless of whether I live or die. They didn't shut me up; they gave me a pulpit! Alive, I'm Christ's messenger; dead I'm His bounty. Life versus even *more* life! I can't lose" (Philippians 1:21-22, TM).

What are you going to do with a man like this? He's beyond your reach! His strength comes from within and is not diminished by the things that surround him.

Everybody wants what successful people have. *The problem is, most of us don't want to do what they did in order to get it.* When it comes to success there's no carpet on the racetrack, and no bed of roses on the battlefield.

The fight begins the moment your eyes open and your feet hit the floor!

Did you know that Lord Nelson, England's famous hero of the sea, struggled with seasickness all his life? Yet this man who sank Napoleon's fleet refused to let his personal struggles rob him of his destiny. Not only did he learn to live with his weakness—he learned to conquer it day by day!

All of us have our battlegrounds. Everybody you meet is struggling at some level. And while nobody pins a medal on us for winning, *nothing* can diminish the satisfaction of knowing that you didn't quit.

I heard about a boy who had lost his right hand in an accident. When the doctor asked him about his handicap, he replied, "I don't have a handicap; I just don't have a right hand!" Later the doctor discovered that he was one of the leading scorers on his high school basketball team.

It's not what you've lost, it's what you have left that counts!

In San Diego's famous Sea World, you can actually see ducks on roller skates. Honestly. But when you get close to them, you'll notice something—they don't have their hearts in it. You may smile, but a lot of us are like that. Instead of living purpose-driven lives, we just let life *happen* to us.

The Bible is a storybook about people who overcame their weaknesses, and went on to change history. Why? Because they had purpose!

Remember Nehemiah? When he showed up, Jerusalem was in ruins and the people of Israel were prisoners. But he rallied, motivated, and organized them. Fifty-two days later, they washed off their trowels, stowed their gear, and walked away from a newly-finished wall. How did he do it?

1) He had passion! He could hardly sleep at night for picturing the problem and seeing himself solving it. That's what it takes.

2) He could motivate others! What good is your leadership if you can't move others to action, or get anybody to follow you?

3) He had confidence! He may have doubted his own ability, but he never doubted God's. His book is full of prayers—silent ones, short ones, specific ones.

4) He refused to give up! From the time he started mixing the mortar until the day he hung the last gate, his attackers never let up. But he took it: sarcasm, suspicion, gossip, threats, false accusations—you name it. Nothing could move him.

5) He was realistic! He had some of the workers building the wall while others stood guard against attack. He acted without overreacting; he was gracious but unbending. Winners don't just have their head in the heavenlies, they've got their feet planted firmly on the ground.

6) He had the discipline to finish the job! Winners are finishers. When the job loses its luster, they don't go somewhere else; they stay at it "in season and out."

Success is an attitude!

Chuck Swindoll says, "Your mind is a thought factory. It produces thousands of thoughts each day. This factory is controlled by one of two foremen, Mr. Triumph and Mr. Defeat.

"Mr. Triumph specializes in producing reasons why you *can* handle whatever comes your way; why you're more than able to conquer. But Mr. Defeat is an expert at producing reasons why you *can't* succeed, and why you should give in and give up.

"Both are instantly obedient; at your signal they snap to attention. Give a positive signal, and Mr. Triumph will throw the switches and see to it that one encouraging, uplifting thought after another floods your mind. But turn Mr. Defeat loose, and in the name of reality or common sense he'll convince you that you can't, or won't, or shouldn't. He'll drain all your energy, squelch all your confidence, and turn you into a frowning, tight-lipped, fatalistic victim.

"Happiness is not a matter of intelligence, age, or position. No, it's a matter of *right thinking*. Your joy is directly related to the thoughts you've deposited in your memory bank. You can only draw out what you've put in."

What kind of performance would your car give if you kept putting dirt into the gas tank? The same is true of your life.

But you say, "I have so many problems."

You don't have more problems than other people, you just think about them more often! Change how you think and you'll change how you feel!

The apostle Paul writes, "Whatever is true, whatever is noble, whatever is right, whatever is pure, whatever is lovely, whatever is admirable—if anything is excellent or praiseworthy—think about such things . . . and the God of peace will be with you" (Philippians 4:8-9, NIV).

What is your life's goal? What do you dream of accomplishing?

Paul's goal was reaching the world with his message. Listen, "My life is worth nothing unless I use it for doing the work assigned to me" (Acts 20:24, NLT).

Robert Ballard's goal was finding "The Titanic". And he did it. After searching for thirteen years, he found her two miles deep in the Atlantic. How fascinated was he by her? Enough to take 53,000 pictures of her. Enough to study every visible foot of her gigantic frame. Enough to respect her privacy and leave her where he found her—undisturbed and unexploited.

What burns within you? What do you really want?

Do you want to write a book? Begin by putting some thoughts down on paper! Are you wondering if the sacrifice you're making for your children is worth it? It is! Do you want to go back to school? Go; pay the price, even if it takes years! Are you trying to master a skill that takes time, energy, and money? Press on! Are you thinking of going into business or ministry? Step out and do it!

Your heavenly father is creative, and *you're* just like Him. That's why you secretly yearn to do certain things. He put those desires within you!

Refuse to listen to those who've settled for less and want you to do the same!

One hundred and fifty years ago, Martin Van Buren, governor of New York, wrote to President Jackson pointing out the evils of the new railroads. He warned, "Mr. President, railroad carriages are pulled at the enormous speed of 15 mph by engines, which in addition to endangering life and limb of passengers, roar and snort their way through the countryside setting fire to crops, scaring livestock and frightening women and children. The Almighty certainly never intended that people should travel at such break-neck speed."

Can you imagine it? That was the Governor of New York speaking!

Thank God for dreamers; for pioneers who refused to become settlers. We owe them so much. Above my head is an electric light— "Thanks, Tom." On my nose are glasses—"Thanks, Ben." In my driveway is a car—"Thanks, Henry."

Are you getting the idea?

Chapter Eleven

Not Everybody Will Make It

Perhaps you think this chapter title is too negative. Think again: we only change for three reasons. (1) When our pain levels get so high that we're forced to. (2) When what we're doing no longer works for us. (3) When we realize that we *can* change—and become willing to pay the price.

Dick Biggs, a consultant who helps Fortune 500 companies improve profits and increase productivity, writes that all of us have unfair experiences; as a result, some of us adopt a "cease and desist" mentality.

He continues, "One of the best teachers of persistence is your life's critical turning points. Expect to experience three to nine turning points or 'significant changes' in your life. These transitions can be happy experiences . . . or unhappy ones like job losses, divorce, financial setbacks, health problems, or the death of loved ones. But these turning points can also give you a perspective . . . by learning from them, you can actually grow at a deeper level."

James says, "Blessed is the man who perseveres under trial, because when he has stood the test, he will receive the crown" (James 1:12, NIV).

A great illustration of this is the life of Abraham Lincoln.

It reads like the biography of a failure. He had less than one year of formal schooling and failed miserably in business in 1831. He was defeated for the legislature in 1832. He failed again in business a year later. His fiancée died in 1835. He was defeated for Speaker of the House in 1838. He married into what historians call "a living misery" in 1842. Only one of his four sons lived past the age of 18. He was defeated again for Congress in

1843, elected to Congress in 1846, defeated for Congress in 1848, defeated for the Senate in 1855, defeated for Vice President in 1856, defeated for the Senate in 1858—and after 30 years of failure, became one of America's greatest presidents in 1860.

The road to victory is often through multiple defeats.

Without pain and problems our accomplishments have little value! If it costs nothing, it means nothing. Learning to overcome adversity and failure is an inevitable part of achieving success. The key is perseverance. That's why the Psalmist said, "My heart is fixed, Oh God, my heart is fixed" (Psalm 57:7).

There are people who've had it easier than you, and done worse; there are people who've had it harder than you, and done better. The circumstances have very little to do with getting over past failures.

There are four things that keep us all stuck there:

1) Resentment. Quinton Crisp says humorously, "Don't try to keep up with the Joneses, just drag them down to your level—it's cheaper!" Refuse to live a life of comparing, complaining, or criticizing. It's the road to nowhere.

2) Regret. It'll destroy your creative energies and rob you of hope. Don't give place to it. We all have things we wish we'd done better. Forgive yourself and move on.

Recently I read something called *"The City of Regret."* It tells the whole story.

"I had not really planned to take a trip this year, yet I found myself packing anyway. And off I went, dreading it. I was on another guilt trip.

"I booked my reservation on Wish I Had Airlines. I didn't check my bags—everyone carries their own baggage on this airline—and I had to drag mine for what seemed like miles through Regret City Airport. People from all over the world were there too, limping along under the weight of bags they'd packed themselves.

"I caught a cab to Last Resort Hotel, the driver looking back and talking over his shoulder the whole trip. When I got there I found the ballroom where my event would be held; the annual Pity Party.

"As I checked in, I saw that all my old colleagues were on the guest list; the Done family—

Woulda, Coulda, and Shoulda. Both of the Opportunities—Missed and Lost. All of the Yesterdays – there were too many to count, but all would have sad stories to share. Shattered Dreams and Broken Promises would be there, along with their friends, Don't Blame Me and I Can't Help It.

"And of course, hours and hours of entertainment would be provided by that renowned storyteller—*It's Their Fault.*

"As I prepared to settle in for a really long night, I realized that *one person alone* had the power to send all these people back home and break up the party: Me. All I had to do was return to the present and welcome the new day!"

3) Self Pity. Self-pity is deadly. Look at Elijah; twenty-four hours after calling down fire from heaven and single-handedly defeating 850 false prophets, he's wallowing in it. Listen, "I've had enough . . . take away my life . . . I've worked very hard . . . but the people of Israel have broken their covenant with You, and torn down Your altars and killed Your prophets, and only I am left; now they're trying to kill me too" (1 Kings 19:4-10).

There it is—self-pity in the raw. If you give it an inch, it'll take a mile!

Recently I read a story about a parakeet named *Chippie*. The bird's problems began one day when the woman who owned him decided to clean up the dirt and feathers from the bottom of his cage, using a vacuum cleaner. Suddenly the phone rang, she turned to pick it up, and you guessed it, there was an awful sucking sound and—whoosh—Chippie was gone.

In a panic she quickly turned off the vacuum, unzipped the bag, and there was Chippie, stunned, but still breathing. Seeing that he was covered with thick black dust, the owner rushed him to the bathtub, where she turned the water on full blast and held the bird under it. At that point she realized she'd done even more damage, and she quickly cranked up her blow dryer and gave him a blast.

You ask, "How's Chippie doing these days? The answer is, *"OK, but he doesn't sing much anymore."*

What's the moral of the story? Don't let life steal your song!

4) An unteachable spirit. There are just some people who can't be helped. God can't help them and you can't help them either. Here are six of them:

a)   Those who continue to make excuses!
Excuses are generally a crutch for the uncommitted, or a smoke-screen for self-defense. You can't help somebody until they become willing to accept personal responsibility and real solutions. Furthermore, if they won't listen to God, they probably won't listen to you either.

b)   Those who refuse to disconnect from the wrong company! Listen, "Bad company corrupts good character" (1 Corinthians 15:33, NLT). Certain people don't belong in our lives, and nothing good will happen for us until we break the link that connects us to them. My Mom used to say, "If you run with dogs, you'll catch fleas!" Your company will shape your conduct, your conduct will shape your character, and your character will ultimately shape your destiny.

c)   Those who blame God for their problems! One of America's wealthiest men became a self-confessed atheist because he blamed God for letting his sister die. How sad. God is too good to do anything evil and too wise to do anything foolish. There are some things He just stamps, "Will explain later." Until then, you must learn to trust Him. But you'll never see God as your solution, until you stop seeing Him as your problem. Moses said to the children of Israel, "I have set before you life and death, blessing and cursing: therefore choose life" (Deuteronomy 30:19). The choice is always yours!

d) *Those who want to talk, but not listen!* James says there are two kinds of people—hearers and doers. Listen, "Be ye doers of the word, and not hearers only, deceiving your own selves" (James 1:22). If people want what they don't have, they must be willing to do what they haven't done. Furthermore, you're not supposed to keep meeting everybody's needs; you're just supposed to connect them to the One who can. Ultimately they should be dependent on God and themselves—not you.

e) *Those who don't think you're qualified to help them!* Jesus was not recognized in His own hometown, yet He was what they needed. Opportunity doesn't knock, it just stands by waiting to be recognized. If people are "selective" about who they'll receive help from, it's usually because they're not ready to deal with their problem yet.

f) *Those who want what you have but not what you know!* These people want to be rescued but not disciplined; comforted but not confronted. If you keep bailing them out instead of teaching them how to live, you're not doing them any favors. David said, "It was good for me to be afflicted ...that I might learn" (Psalm 119:71 - NIV). Usually we have to taste the pain of what's wrong, before we can appreciate the wisdom of what's right.

John Maxwell says, "The problems of people's past impact them in one of two ways; they experience either a breakdown or a breakthrough."

Sister Francis Cabrini chose the latter.

Chapter Twelve

Refuse to Quit

In 1889 Sister Francis Cabrini got off the boat at Ellis Island. She was 38 years of age. Her goal was to establish an orphanage and a school in New York City. *Had she been consulting her past in order to determine her future, she'd never have left her home in Italy.*

Francesca Lodi-Cabrini was born two months premature in Sant' Angelo, Italy, and she was the sickliest child in her village. At six years of age she decided she wanted to become a missionary to China. But people mocked her dream. "A missionary order would never accept a girl who is ill most of the time," her sister Rosa told her.

When she reached the required age of eighteen, she applied to join a convent and was indeed rejected because she was too sickly. But rejection was not going to make her give up her dream of ministering in Asia.

She began doing what she could where she lived, to build up her strength and prove her worth. She taught neighborhood children. She cared for an older villager. When a smallpox epidemic hit, she nursed family and friends through it until she herself became sick. When she recovered, she reapplied to the convent—and was turned down again.

Six years later she finally gained acceptance.

She thought that would put her one step closer to achieving her dream. But she was to experience many more setbacks. Both her parents died within a year. Then she was assigned to teach at a local school rather than one overseas. When she applied to other organizations devoted to working in Asia, they rejected her too. Next, she was asked to oversee a small orphanage in Codogno, a town not more than fifty miles from her home. She spent the next six frustrating years there, until the orphanage was finally closed down.

When she still dreamed of traveling to Asia, a superior told her that if she wanted to be part of a missionary order, she should start one herself. So that's what she did. With the assistance of a half-dozen girls from the orphanage, she founded the Missionary Sisters of the Sacred Heart in 1880. During the next eight years, she built the order, establishing foundations in Milan, Rome, and other Italian cities.

Still she kept trying to earn a place in Asia.

However, Pope Leo XIII put an end to her dream by telling her, "Not to the East, but to the West. You will find a vast field of labor in the United States." She was to help run an orphanage, a school, and a convent in New York City.

That is how Sister Frances Cabrini came to Ellis Island in March, 1889.

She left her lifelong dream behind her in ruins in Italy. But she didn't look back, nor did she allow the past to hold her hostage.

For the next twenty-eight years, she dedicated herself to the task of ministering to people in the Americas. And she overcame plenty of obstacles to do it. When she arrived in New York, she was told that the plans for the orphanage, school, and convent had fallen through and that she should return to Italy.

Instead, she solved the problems they were having , and established the facilities anyway.

It didn't matter what difficulties she faced, she continually overcame them. *By the time she died in 1917, at age 87, she had founded more than 70 hospitals, schools, and orphanages, in the United States, Spain, France, England, and South America.*

Her impact was incredible. She was the Mother Teresa of her day—possessing similar compassion, grit, tenacity, and leadership.

But she never would have made a difference if she had allowed her past to hold her hostage. Instead of lamenting the loss of her dream and the hurts of her youth, she moved on and did what she could where God put her.

You can do the same.

Chapter Thirteen

Taking Risks

Jesus, the greatest of all teachers, said, "Everyone who asks receives; he who seeks finds; and to him who knocks, the door will be opened" (Matthew 7:7, NIV). So often we lose when we could have won, because we were afraid to keep asking, to keep seeking, and to keep knocking.

We just stood back and let somebody else take the risk—and get the reward.

Some time ago I read these powerful words: "To laugh is to risk appearing a fool. To weep is to risk appearing sentimental. To reach out to another is to risk involvement. To expose your feelings to others is to risk rejection. To place your dreams before the crowd is to risk ridicule. To love is to risk not being loved in return. To go forward in the face of overwhelming odds, is to risk failure. But risks must be taken because the greatest risk of all is to risk nothing. The person who risks nothing, does nothing, has nothing, and is nothing. He may avoid suffering and sorrow, but he cannot learn, he cannot feel, he cannot change, he cannot grow, and he cannot love. Chained by his certitudes he is a slave. *Only the person who risks is truly free."*

David Bayles and Ted Orland tell about a ceramics teacher, who created a unique grading system for his students. Here's how it worked.

He divided the class into two groups. The first group would be graded solely on the *number* of pieces they produced, and the second group on the *quality* of the pieces they produced. The procedure was simple. The teacher would weigh the work of the first group. Fifty pounds of ceramic pots rated an "A," forty pounds a "B," and so on.

Those being graded strictly on *quality* needed to produce only one pot—but it had to be as near perfect as possible to get an "A."

The results were amazing. The first group got busy churning out pots— each of them better than the one before. But the second group just sat around talking about perfection, and in the end had nothing to show for their efforts but grandiose theories— and a pile of dead clay.

What a lesson! Until you overcome your fear of making a mistake, you'll never make anything. You'll certainly never make much of a difference.

Time Magazine did a feature on a group of people who had lost their jobs *three times* because of plant closings. Psychologists expected them to be discouraged, but they were surprisingly optimistic. Their adversity had actually created an advantage! Because they had *already* lost a job and found a new one at least twice, they were *better able* to handle adversity than people who had worked for only one company and suddenly found themselves unemployed.

Lloyd Ogilvie tells of an acquaintance who was a trapeze artist. The man described learning to work on the trapeze this way:

"When you finally understand that the net will always catch you, you stop worrying about falling. But it takes repeated falls to convince you of that. However, once you know that, you can begin to concentrate on catching the bar, learning the techniques, and developing confidence. When that happens, you fall less—*and each fall makes you able to risk more.*"

Don't be afraid of "blowing it." You can't advance without going through difficulties; you simply can't do it! And even if you could, you'd have nothing to share with others that they could relate to.

In 1978, Bernie Marcus, the son of a poor Russian cabinetmaker in Newark, was fired from Handy Dan, a do-it-yourself hardware retailer.

Getting fired is traumatic for even the best of us, for it can mean the loss of security, identity, and self-worth. In reality, it can be as painful as the loss of a marriage or a loved one.

But instead of giving up, Marcus teamed up with a friend and they started their own business. In 1979 they opened their first store in Atlanta, Georgia. It was called the *Home Depot*.

Today, they have more than 760 stores employing over 157,000 people, and the business has now expanded overseas. Each year his corporation does more than *30 billion dollars* worth of sales.

Now I doubt if Bernie Marcus enjoyed getting fired, but look what he'd have missed if he hadn't!

University of Houston professor, Jack Matson, recognized that in order to succeed you must first learn to deal with failure. So he developed a course for his students called *Failure 101*. In class he got his students to build mock-ups of products that nobody would ever buy. *His goal was to get them to equate failure with creativity—instead of defeat.* That way they freed themselves to keep trying new things without fear.

Some of the world's greatest success stories resulted from what seemed like mistakes at the time.

Kellogg's Corn Flakes were created because boiled wheat was accidentally left baking in a pan overnight. Ivory Soap floats because a batch of it was left in a mixer too long, and air got whipped into it. Paper towels were invented because a machine put too many layers of tissue together. Horace Walpole said, "In science, mistakes always precede the truth."

Success in any field is always preceded by mistakes, discoveries, and the courage that turns obstacles into opportunities. When you can accept that and work with it, the future is yours.

Chapter Fourteen

Don't Limit Your Potential

Until Roger Bannister showed up, the world believed that *nobody* could break the 4-minute mile. People thought, "If it hasn't been done, it's because it can't be." Wrong! Bannister not only did it; he started a new trend.

Did you know that the 1936 Olympic world records have now become the *qualifying* standards for today's athletes. Why? Because now we *know* we can do better!

Have you ever seen trained fleas? When you first put them in the jar and put the lid on it, they jump up and down, frantically hitting their heads against it. But finally, after a lot of headaches, they quit jumping so high and enjoy their newfound comfort. At this point you can remove the lid and the fleas will still be held captive; not by a real lid, but by a mindset that says, *"So high and no higher."*

Do voices in your head say the same thing to you?

Why don't we bounce back? Why don't we get up and try again? For several reasons. First, we don't want to be embarrassed or look bad. How many times did you fall before you learned to walk? How often did you garble your language before you learned to speak properly?

Sometimes we refuse to try again because we're waiting and hoping that things will get easier. If Michelangelo had been looking for the easy way out, he would have painted *the floor* of the Sistine Chapel instead of the ceiling—and his life's work would have been lost forever.

You've got to pay the price. Listen to the words of the master teacher: "For which one of you when he wants to build a tower, does not first sit down and calculate the cost?" (Luke 14:28, NAS).

What are you waiting for—the perfect time? Instead of waiting for life to happen, go out and make it happen!

Someone once asked Oscar Wilde, the playwright, what the difference was between an amateur and a professional. He replied, "An amateur writes when he feels like it; a professional writes regardless."

Microsoft magnate Bill Gates says, "When you get an insight or an inspiration, do something about it within the first 24 hours—or the odds are against your *ever* doing it."

When Gates started out, most people, including some of his friends, dismissed him as "a geek." Why? Because he dared to think "outside the box" and to go where nobody had ever gone before. Furthermore, he took the risk of sinking every penny he had into his dream, including what he could borrow.

It paid off—today he's one of the five richest men on earth!

Fletcher Byrom says, "Make sure you generate a reasonable number of mistakes. Too many executives are so *afraid* of error that they rigidify the organization with checks and counterchecks, discourage innovation, and in the end, so structure themselves that they miss the kind of offbeat opportunity that can send a company skyrocketing."

Whether you're trying to rebuild your life, your marriage, or your career, you'll *always* have to deal with fear; it's just that your fear will be different at 90 than it is at 19. Once you accept that, you'll feel less unique and alone.

Did you know that Julius Caesar conquered the world, but was terrified of thunder? Or that Peter the Great of Russia cried like a child when he had to cross bridges? Doctor Samuel Johnson, the celebrated British writer, was afraid to enter a room with his left foot first. If he did accidentally, he backed out and re-entered with his right one.

Refuse to let fear control your life or it'll keep you from reaching your destiny. What a price! Remember again the words of John Maxwell, "Fear breeds inaction, inaction breeds lack of experience, lack of experience breeds ignorance, and ignorance breeds fear."

If you're caught in this deadly cycle, here are some "fear-fighters" on which you need to meditate regularly, and commit to memory.

1) "Have not I commanded thee? Be strong and of a good courage; be not afraid, neither be thou dismayed; for the Lord thy God is with thee whithersoever thou goest" (Joshua 1:9).

2) "For God hath not given us the spirit of fear, but of power, and of love, and of a sound mind" (2 Timothy 1:7). Note: fear is a spirit—an attitude—a response pattern.

3) "Thou wilt keep him in perfect peace, whose mind is stayed on Thee; because he trusteth in Thee" (Isaiah 26:3). My friend, Sarah Utterbach, says, "He can't be your peace unless He is first your focus."

4) "For the Lord. . . He it is that doth go before thee; He will be with thee, He will not fail thee, neither forsake thee; fear not, neither be dismayed" (Deuteronomy 31:8).

5) "In God I have put my trust; I will not fear what flesh can do unto me" (Psalm 56:4).

6) "Peace I leave with you, My peace I give unto you: not as the world giveth, give I unto you. Let not your heart be troubled, neither let it be afraid" (John 14:27).

7) "For He hath said I will never leave thee nor forsake thee. So that we may boldly say, the Lord is my helper . . . I will not fear what man shall do unto me" (Hebrews 13:5-6).

When God gives you an idea, or speaks to you with definite direction—*that's the moment of truth!*

At that very moment you either make a commitment or make an excuse. You act in faith or react in fear; but right then you're deciding your future.

Fear usually comes dressed up as an excuse. Every time you pull back from a God-given opportunity because of fear, you lay one more brick in the wall that will ultimately keep you from reaching your life's goals.

If God has opened a door for you, just take His hand and start moving forward. You can't control the wind, but by His grace you can adjust your sails to take you where you want to go.

Remember, opportunity is a visitor; don't assume it will be back again tomorrow. Move while the door is open!

Chapter Fifteen

What's Your Achilles Heel?

Achilles was a mythological Greek warrior, who was supposed to be indestructible—except for one tiny spot on his heel. And that's the spot that destroyed him.

We refer to these areas as our "blind spots."

Sometimes we're blind to our *strengths,* and go through life thinking others are wiser or more worthy than we are. As a result we miss a lot of great things we could have had.

But more often than not, our blind spots are in the area of our *weaknesses.* Ego can blind us to our own vulnerability. If you're unwilling to acknowledge that you've got a problem, you won't protect yourself in that area or work on it, and as a result you'll keep getting into trouble.

Here are five very common reasons why we fail:

First, we fail because we love things more than people.

People don't care how much you know, until they first know how much you care. The truth is, when others think you don't really care about them, they can actually *help* you to fail, or at least stand by and do nothing to keep it from happening. On the other hand, you can survive a lot of mistakes because people remember your kindness. Jesus said, "Blessed are the merciful: for they shall obtain mercy" (Matthew 5:7). It's the harvest law and it still works today.

Are you "up front" with people or do they have to wonder about your motives? Do you listen when they talk, or are you just waiting for your turn to speak? Do you expect everybody to conform to your wishes, your schedule, and your agenda, or do you look for ways to help and accommodate them?

Recently I read an article entitled "How to Prevent Organizational Dry Rot." It's a real eye opener, especially if you're a leader of any kind.

1) Have an effective program for the recruitment and development of talent; people are the ultimate source of renewal.

2) Don't kill the spark of individuality.

3) Cultivate a climate where it's comfortable to ask questions.

4) Don't carve the internal structure in stone; most structures are designed to solve problems that no longer exist.

5) Have a good system of internal communication.

6) Don't become prisoners of procedures. In most organizations, the rulebook grows fatter as the ideas grow fewer.

7) Combat tendencies toward the vested interest of a few; in the long run everyone's best interest is in the continuing vitality of the group.

8) Be more interested in what you are becoming, than in what you have been.

9) An organization runs on three things; motivation, conviction, and morale; each person

has to believe that his talent means something and that he is recognized by the whole.

10) The profit-and-loss statement is not the true measure of your success; fulfilling your God-given purpose and making daily progress toward your goals is.

Second, we fail because of a negative outlook.

Did you hear about the man who went to the fortune-teller? After studying his palm she said to him, "You'll be sad, miserable, and poor until you're thirty." He asked, "What happens when I'm thirty?" She replied, "Then you'll get used to it!"

It happens so easily, especially in the company of the wrong people. Before you know it, you're criticizing and complaining again, and the atmosphere around you is negative. Why? Because *your words* create the climate you live in. Furthermore, healthy people won't live in that climate.

But you say, "I only talk like that when I'm upset." Listen, "Do not be anxious about anything, but . . . *with thanksgiving* present your requests to God. And the peace of God, which transcends all understanding, will guard your hearts" (Philippians 4:6-7, NIV).

Did you get that? You free yourself from anxiety by thanksgiving—not by complaining. Never let the level of your thanksgiving be according to your circumstances, for God is *greater* than any circumstance.

You say, how do I change?

1) You have to want to. Abraham Lincoln said, "Most folks are about as happy as they make up their minds to be."

2) Catch yourself in the act. If you've always been negative, don't expect to change overnight. But make a start; from now on if you can't say something helpful, say nothing.

3) Begin to look for what's good—and you'll find it. Listen, "Whatever is true . . . noble . . . right . . . pure . . . lovely . . . think about such things" (Philippians 4:8, NIV).

Third, we fail is because we're in the wrong place.

Often failure is just a result of mismatched abilities, interests, personalities, or values. Think about that carefully.

Business consultant Paul Stokes maintains that the most important ingredient in success is in being able to identify your mountain, or your purpose in life. He says, "I run into people every day who are basically climbing the wrong mountain. They've spent twenty years or more doing something that has no real purpose for them. Then one day they look back and say, 'What have I been doing?'"

Is that how you feel today?

Before you start the journey, check the roadmap. Ask God for direction. His promise is, "In all thy ways acknowledge Him, and He shall direct thy paths" (Proverbs 3:6). God has a plan and a purpose for your life.

You have nothing—absolutely nothing—more important to do, than find that plan and fulfill it.

Fourth, we fail because of a lack of commitment.

Goethe said, "Until you are committed there is a hesitance, a chance to draw back, and always ineffectiveness. But the moment you commit yourself, a whole stream of events result from that decision, bringing in your favor unforeseen incidents and material assistance which nobody could have dreamed would come his way."

The last time you failed, did you stop trying because you failed, or did you fail because you stopped trying?

Jessie Owens set his first world record in junior high school. Then in college he broke three world records in less than an hour. In 1936, he showed his real character at the Olympics in Nazi Germany. As Hitler watched, he set three more world records, and won four gold medals. Losing to a black American was more than Hitler could stand, and he stormed out of the stadium in a rage.

Later Jessie Owens wrote: *"There is something that can happen to every athlete and every human being; the instinct to slack off. To give in to pain, to give less than your best . . . the instinct to hope you can win through luck, or through your opponent not doing his best, instead of going to the limit and past the limit, where victory is always found. Defeating those negative instincts that are out to defeat us, is the difference between winning and losing—and we face that battle every day of our lives."*

Those words should be posted where you can read them every day!

God is not limited by your limitations. He used a boy's slingshot to bring down a giant, and a teenage girl named Esther to save her nation from a holocaust. God's neither dependent on what you have, nor limited by what you don't have.

Paul says, "God deliberately chose . . . things counted as nothing at all, and used them . . . so that no one can ever boast" (1 Corinthians 1:27-29, NLT). Jesus said, "I will build my church" (Matthew 16:18). Build it with what? Twelve people just like you and me. But when He poured Himself into them, He was so *concentrated* in them, that if two of them got together, they could turn any town upside down.

But you say, "I have so many weaknesses." We all come to the Lord damaged and in need of repair. But just because you're damaged doesn't mean you're not delivered. No, it just means you're not yet fully developed. You can be delivered in one area and struggling in another—yet God will still use you for His glory.

Years ago, T. D. Jakes preached his famous sermon, Woman Thou Art Loosed, to a Bible class of *forty* women in West Virginia. In those days no one had ever heard of him. But he remained faithful, teachable, and available to God. Last year he preached that same sermon to *86,000 women in the Georgia Dome!*

Your limited education, your obscurity, your race, and even your past failures will not stop you—but your lack of commitment will!

Fifth, we fail because of our inability or unwillingness to change.

Whether it's an organization or an individual, we all struggle with this one.

Recently I smiled as I read the "Top Ten Strategies for Dealing with a Dead Horse." Check and see if you recognize any of them:

1) Buy a stronger whip.

2) Change riders.

3) Appoint a committee to study the horse.

4) Find a team to revive the horse.

5) Send out a memo declaring the horse really isn't dead.

6) Hire an expensive consultant and find "the real problem."

7) Harness several dead horses together for increased speed and efficiency.

8) Rewrite the standard definition for a live horse.

9) Declare the horse to be better, faster, and cheaper when dead.

10) Promote the horse to a supervisory position.

Change can be painful, especially if you've been doing things a certain way for a long time. Furthermore, it often means leaving behind people who are not willing to move forward.

But *that's* the cost of personal growth and success!

Sometimes changing and growing means finding a mentor. I simply wouldn't be where I am today without mentors, especially in those early years when I had little training, and even less direction.

My first mentor taught me that without the discipline to read, I had no future. He'd say, "Until you have water in your own well, you've got to draw it from other men's wells." Then he taught me which ones to draw it from.

In those days I was a traveling speaker, so he was very demanding about things like personal appearance, hygiene, and good manners, especially when I was a guest in someone's home. He was a real stickler for study habits and the development of vocabulary. He'd say, "Words paint pictures. People need to *see* it as well as *hear* it."

At times I felt like he was being hard on me, but now I realize that he was just what I needed. Why? Because he knew how to love, but not over-protect; to stretch, but not beyond the breaking point; to encourage, but not overindulge, to release, but never abandon. What a gift Dr. Gordon Magee was to me.

In this day of tarnished leaders, busy parents, and arrogant authority figures, we need more mentors like him—guides who know they're not gods. Coaches behind the scenes who know how to whisper both hope and reproof on our journey toward excellence. Do you have a mentor?

Your future could depend on it.

Chapter Sixteen

The Difference Is Attitude!

One night when Thomas Edison was 67 years old, he watched as most of his life's work burned to the ground. Standing in the ashes he turned to a friend and said, *"Thank goodness all of our mistakes are burned up. Now we can start again fresh."*

You can start again. You can begin your life all over again today, if you want too. John Maxwell writes, "Each time you plan, risk, fail, re-evaluate, and adjust, you have another opportunity to begin again, only better than the last time.

"Every time you face mistakes and attempt to move forward in spite of them, is a test of character.

"There always comes a time when giving up is easier than standing up, and giving in looks more attractive than digging in. In those moments, *character* may be the only thing you have to draw on to keep you going."

Championship-winning NBA coach Pat Riley said, "There comes a moment that defines winning from losing. The true warrior understands and seizes the moment by giving an effort so intensive and intuitive that it could be called one from the heart."

After you've been knocked down and had the will to get back up, the intelligence to plan your comeback, and the courage to take action, know this: you will experience one of those defining moments. And it will define you—as an achiever or a quitter. Prepare for that moment and know that it's coming—and you'll increase your chances of winning your way through it.

But let me point out something very important right here.

It's not enough just to stay in the ring. That's commendable, but if that's all you do, you'll get your brains knocked out and still not win. The secret is to get back up and do things *differently* next time. Aldous Huxley said, "Experience is not what happens to you. Experience is what you *do* with what happens to you." Think about that carefully.

Have you ever written down your goals? If you don't know where you're going, any road will get you there. It's your goals that determine your strategy. It works like this: your goal determines your plan, your plan determines your actions, and your actions determine your success.

Here are some wise words from an old prophet that you need to ponder: "Write the vision, and make it plain . . . that he may run that readeth it" (Habakkuk 2:2). Write down your goal on a 3x5 card. Carry it with you wherever you go. Read it daily. It'll keep you from losing your way. Remember, busyness and barrenness go hand in hand, so before you hit the throttle—check the compass.

Novelist Victor Hugo said, "He who every morning plans the transactions of the day and follows that plan, carries a thread that will guide him through the labyrinth of the most busy life. But where no plan is laid, where the disposal of time is surrendered merely to chance, chaos will soon reign."

Benjamin Franklin bottom-lined it: "By failing to plan, you are planning to fail."

But once you have a plan of action, you need the right *attitude*. We're talking here about a spirit that never gives up!

I'm fascinated by the life of Thomas Edison. Anybody who can give the world the electric light, the microphone, the storage battery, the phonograph, and a thousand other inventions, is worth studying. Historians say he was driven by one word: purpose. *Not pleasure, not popularity, not even personal gain—but purpose.*

Here are some of the recorded principles by which he lived: 1) Work to obtain all the knowledge you can about what you want to achieve. 2) Fix your mind on your purpose. Persist! Seek! Use all the knowledge you can accumulate or learn from others. 3) Keep on searching no matter how many times you meet with disappointment. 4) Refuse to be influenced by the fact that someone else tried the same thing and failed. 5) Keep yourself *sold* on the idea that a solution to the problem exists somewhere, and that you'll find it.

Then he adds, "The trouble with most people is, they quit before they ever start."

It's only when you've done your part that you can call on God with confidence to do the things you can't do. Nehemiah didn't conquer through brilliance, he conquered through prayer—*and perseverance* (Nehemiah 4:9). In spite of the criticism, in spite of the pressure, he refused to fold his tent and run—that's why he rebuilt Jerusalem.

God *always* honors the man or the woman with a spirit that never gives up—*always!* So take another look at your attitude. Do a check-up from the neck-up!

Chapter Seventeen

Keep Playing!

One night, before a huge audience, the great violinist Paganini stood before a huge audience playing a difficult piece of music. A full orchestra surrounded him. Suddenly one of the strings on his violin broke and hung down from his instrument. Beads of perspiration formed on his brow, but he continued to play, improvising as he went.

To everybody's surprise a second string broke. Then a third. Now there were three limp strings dangling from his violin, as the master performer completed the composition on the one remaining string. When he was through, the audience jumped to its feet and filled the hall with thunderous applause. When the clapping and shouting ceased, Paganini asked the audience to sit down.

Holding the violin high for everyone to see, he nodded to the conductor to begin the encore. Then turning back toward the crowd, with a twinkle in his eye he smiled and shouted, *"Paganini...and one string!"*

With his Stradivarius beneath his chin he played the final piece while the audience and the conductor shook their heads in amazement.

Paganini...and one string...and an attitude that refuses to quit.

That's what it takes!

The inspiring Victor Frankl, who was a prisoner during the Holocaust, endured years of indignity and humiliation before he was finally liberated.

When he was first captured he was marched into a Gestapo courtroom. His captors had taken away his home, his family, his freedom, his possessions, and even his watch and wedding ring. After shaving his head and stripping him, he stood naked under the glaring lights of the German High Command, being interrogated and falsely accused. He was destitute, a helpless pawn in the hands of brutal, prejudiced men.

But in that moment something happened to him. He suddenly realized there was one thing nobody could ever take from him—just one.

The power to choose his own attitude!

Regardless of what anyone did to him, or what the future held for him, he could always choose his own attitude. Bitterness or forgiveness. To give up or go on. Hatred or hope. Determination to endure, or the paralysis of self-pity. *It all boiled down to "Frankl...and one string!"*

The longer I live the more I believe that life is about 10% of what happens to us and 90% of how we respond to it.

The most important decision you'll make every day is your choice of an attitude. It's more important than your past, your education, your wealth, what other people think about you, your circumstances, or your position. Attitude is the "single string" that either keeps you going or cripples your progress. With the right attitude, no barrier is too high, no valley is too deep, no goal is too extreme, and no challenge is too great.

Yet we spend more of our time fretting over the strings that snap—things we can't change— than we do giving attention to the one that remains, our choice of attitude.

Remember the *Serenity Prayer?* It goes like this:

"God grant me the serenity to accept the things I cannot change, the courage to change the things I can, and the wisdom to know the difference."

Unless we are willing to pray that prayer and live by it's principles, we suffer, grow sour, get ulcers, and become twisted. Some of us actually die because of it.

Dozens of studies have confirmed that. One study called "Broken Heart" researched the death rate of 4,500 widowers within six months of the deaths of their wives. Compared with other men of the same age, these widowers had a mortality rate—40% higher. *Why? Because they gave up!*

Harold Kushner, an army medical officer held by the Viet Cong for over five years, tells of a soldier who died because of his *attitude*. In an article in *New York* Magazine, this tragic account is told:

"Among the prisoners in Kushner's POW camp, was a tough young marine twenty-four years old. He had already survived two years of prison-camp life in relatively good health. Part of the reason for this was because the camp commander had promised to release him if he cooperated. Since this had been done before with others, he turned into a model POW and even became the leader of the camp's 'thought-reform group.'

"But as time passed he realized they had lied to him. When the full realization of that took hold, he became a zombie. He refused to do all work, rejected all offers of food and encouragement, and simply lay on his cot sucking his thumb. In a matter of weeks he was dead."

When that last string snapped, there was nothing left!

Chapter Eighteen

Be Relentless!

For a just man falleth seven times, and riseth up again. (Proverbs 24:16)

The theme of Christianity is—rising again! King Solomon says a just man is successful because he *continues* to get up. God will enable you to stand in the midst of contrary winds, and when you stumble, to grasp the hand of His grace and get back up one more time. Listen: "They that stumbled are girded with strength" (1 Samuel 2:4).

If you want to accomplish anything of significance, then you must be relentless! Relentless people refuse to take "no" for an answer. They try things one way, and if that doesn't work, they try them another. But they never give up!

You, who are about to break beneath the weight of your struggles, be relentless! Don't give up on your family! Don't give up on your business! Don't give up on yourself!

A terrible thing happens when you give up; it's called regret. It's the nagging thought, "If only I'd tried harder, or tried again, maybe—just maybe—I could have succeeded."

In the 14th century the Emperor Tamerlane, a descendant of Genghis Khan, was badly defeated in battle. As he lay hidden in a barn, enemy troops scoured the countryside looking for him. Suddenly he noticed an ant trying to push a kernel of corn that was many times bigger than itself, up over a wall. *Sixty-nine* times the ant tried and failed, but on the seventieth try, it succeeded. Leaping to his feet Tamerland shouted, "If you can do it, I can too!"

He reorganized his forces, went back and soundly defeated the enemy!

If you're thinking of quitting, listen to the words of General Joab, who led King David's armies: "Be strong and let us fight bravely . . . the LORD will do what is good" (2 Samuel 10:12, NIV).

Joab knew that if you do your part, God will do the rest. *As long as you are on the battlefield God can give your victory. But if you quit, what more can He do for you?*

Never give up when you know you're right! *Believe* that all things work together for good, if you just persevere! *Don't* let the odds discourage you, God is bigger than all of them. *Refuse* to let anybody intimidate you or deter you from your goals! *Fight* and overcome every limitation! *Remember*, every winner has dealt with defeat and adversity!

In a recent survey of very successful people, not one of them viewed their mistakes as failures. They simply called them learning experiences or tuition paid, or opportunities for growth. What an attitude!

Henry Ward Beecher said, "It takes defeat to turn bone into flint, gristle into muscle, and make us invincible. It forms in us that heroic nature that causes us to rise above all obstacles. Don't be afraid of defeat, for you are never so near to victory as when you are defeated in a good cause."

Did you notice the words, "so near to victory"? *That's* where you are today!

Come on, get back up. Try one more time. The next time can be the last time; the time when you break through!

What do you really want? To break a habit? To make your marriage work? To lose weight? To get out of debt? To get over your hurts and move on? To start your own business? To become more patient, loving, and gracious? To spend more time with your children or your mate? To learn the computer? To go back to church? To take a trip? Go ahead, *you* fill in the blank: _____.

Now listen to these words: "By His mercies we have been kept from complete destruction . . . His mercies begin afresh each day; great is Your faithfulness;" (Lamentations 3:22-23 - NLT).

It's a new day. You are being offered a chance to start over. Take hold of God's hand. Stand on His promise. Receive His strength. Believe that this time, by His grace, you—will—succeed!